Meet the Author

Meet Elizabeth Kollmar—rubber band crafter, author, and eleven year old! Elizabeth has always been super crafty and full of ideas. Her creative thinking led to the design of the twelve motifs and countless variations you'll find in this book. Find out more about Elizabeth and the things she loves...

What kind of crafts do you like?

My family is very creative and we love fiber arts. I learned the basics of knitting and crochet when I was very little by doing lots of projects with my family. I even designed my own knitting piece when I was six!

How did you start working with rubber bands?

My mom works at a craft store, so we knew when rubber bands were getting to be a big thing. So many other kids my age were using rubber band looms to make cool projects. I wanted to try it out to see what I could do.

Why do you use a hook?

My mom bought my brother, sister, and me a rubber band loom before we left for vacation. We wouldn't be able to use the Internet while we were away, so we wrote down a few instructions for the loom before we left. I just couldn't get them to work for me, so I started playing with the hook that came with the loom. Because I knew a little bit about crochet, it seemed natural for me to loop the bands on the hook. The only problem was I had to take the bands off the hook to turn them around and work on the other side. Getting the bands on and off the hook was really tricky, but then my mom suggested I use a double-ended crochet hook so I wouldn't have to take them off at all. It was perfect!

What other hobbies do you have?

I love photography. I've competed in some junior competitions and won a few first place awards! I also like reading and music. I play the piano and the harp.

What do you do when you're not crafting?

I love outdoor activities like horseback riding, bicycling, swimming, and archery. My family has lots of small pets that I help take care of. My favorite is my Dutch bunny named Emily. I also spend lots of time having fun with my parents and older brother and younger sister. We love doing special things together.

What do you want to do when you grow up?

My dream job is one where I can care for or train animals!

Where can I find out more about you and your work?

Visit me at *elizabethkollmar.com* to learn about my current projects and activities.

Look What You Can Make!

Baby Leaf
Page 19

Rainy Day
Page 21

Rolling Waves
Page 24

Vining Leaves
Page 27

Half Shell
Page 29

Strawberries
Page 34

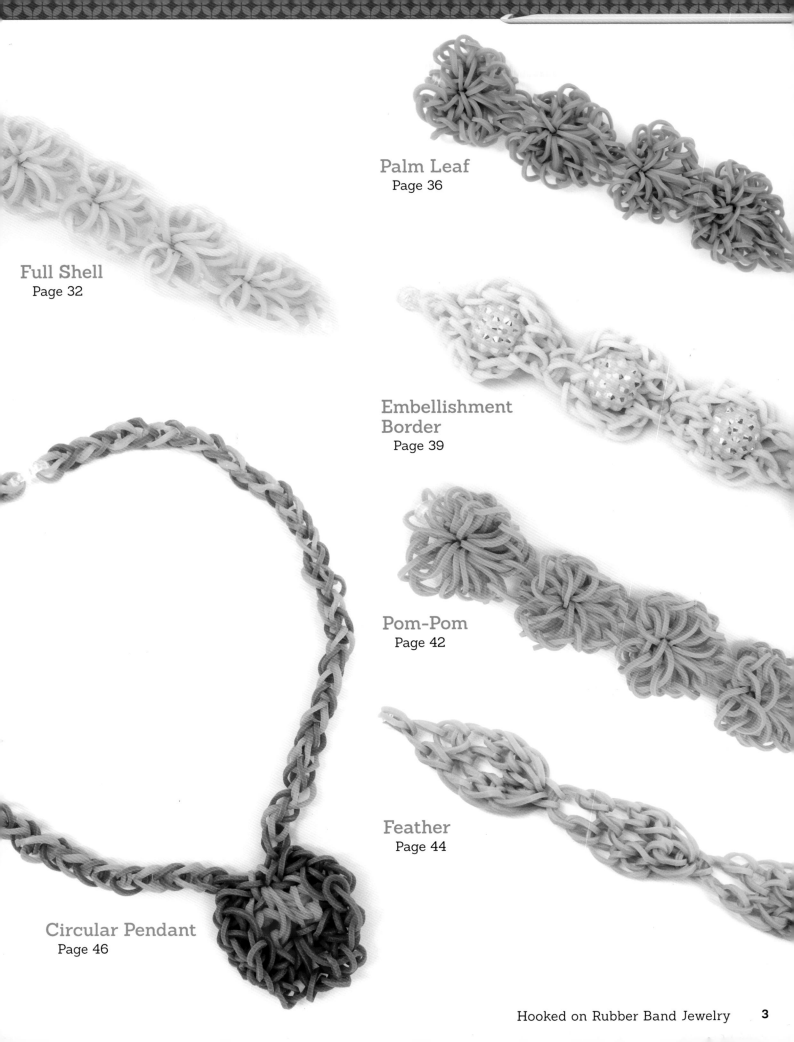

Full Shell
Page 32

Palm Leaf
Page 36

Embellishment Border
Page 39

Pom-Pom
Page 42

Feather
Page 44

Circular Pendant
Page 46

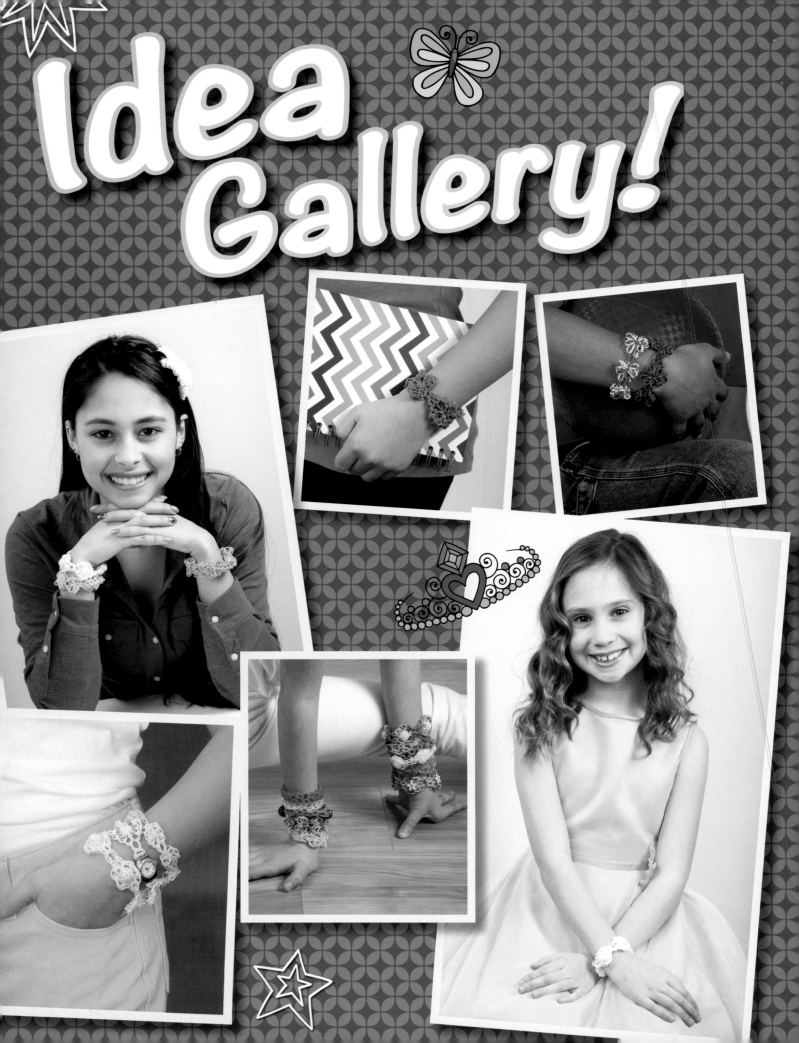

Idea Gallery!

How to Use This Book

This book uses a very unique method of banding, but don't worry—it's easy! Here, you'll find everything you need to know to achieve success!

The instructions and diagrams will show you how to make different design motifs that you can repeat to craft things like bracelets and necklaces. All of the motifs contain the same elements so you can follow along easily:

- ★ Difficulty level
- ★ Gauge
- ★ Materials list: What Do I Need?
- ★ Instructions: Breaking the Code!
- ★ Diagrams

Difficulty Level

This is just a guide to let you know how complicated a project is before you get started. If you're new to banding, try starting with a beginner motif and move up to intermediate and advanced motifs as you gain skills and confidence.

Gauge

The gauge tells you how long a motif is when it is not being stretched. You can use the gauge (plus a tape measure and calculator) to figure out how many times you need to repeat a motif to make a project the length you want. Once you figure out the number of motifs you need to make, you can figure out how many bands you need for your project. Figuring out the number of bands ahead of time means you won't have to run out to the store to get more while you're making your project! See the example on page 7 to figure out how to calculate the number of motifs and bands you need to make a project.

What is a motif?

A motif is a single design that can be repeated several times to create a piece of jewelry or other item. Many motifs, like the one at the right, are built from the bottom up.

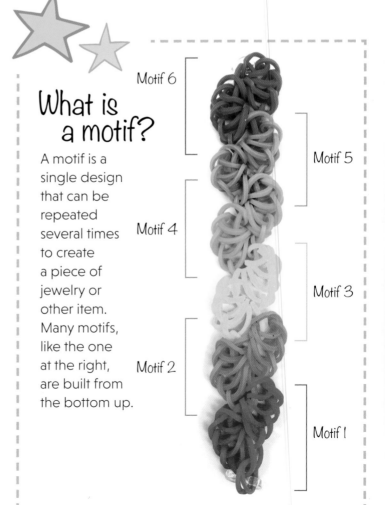

Motif 6

Motif 5

Motif 4

Motif 3

Motif 2

Motif 1

Sizing Example:

Let's figure out how to use the gauge to plan your project. Say you want to make a bracelet. First, measure around your wrist to see how long the bracelet should be. Let's say your wrist measures 6" around. Subtract 1" from this measurement. The result is the finished length you want your bracelet to be. Subtracting an inch will ensure your bracelet fits snugly because the bands will have to stretch just a bit to fit your wrist.

You've calculated the finished length for your bracelet. Now it's time to pick your motif. Say you want to make a bracelet using the Half Shell motif (page 29). The Half Shell motif has a gauge of 1". To figure out the number of motifs you need to make for your bracelet, divide the finished length for your bracelet by the gauge of the motif you want to use. You will need to repeat the motif 5 times to make your bracelet.

The materials list tells you that you need 10 bands to make 1 Half Shell motif. To figure out the number of bands you need for the entire bracelet, multiply the number of motifs you need to make by the number of bands you need for just one motif.

Each project uses foundation bands to get started. Don't forget to add these to the total number of bands for your project. The Half Shell motif uses 2 foundation bands. Add this to the number of bands you calculated in Step 3 above.

Step 1:

wrist measurement		subtract for a snug fit		finished length
6"	−	1"	=	5"

Step 2:

finished length measurement		motif gauge		number of motifs needed
5	÷	1"	=	5

Step 3:

number of motifs needed		number of bands in each motif		number of motif bands needed
5	x	10	=	50

Step 4:

number of motif bands needed		number of foundation bands needed		total number of bands needed
50	+	2		52

Too Short? What if repeating a motif five times is not enough, but repeating it six times is too much? You can always add length to a project by attaching a chain of bands (see page 12) before the first motif and/or after the last motif.

What Do I Need?

Before you get started, you'll want to have these items on hand. They will be easy to find at your local craft or hobby store.

Rubber bands (¾" [2cm] in diameter): The materials list for each motif lists the number of foundation bands you need to get started, plus the number of bands you'll need to make one motif. Follow the example on page 7 to use this info to figure out how many bands you'll need to make your entire project.

Double-ended crochet hook: This is a crochet hook with a hook on both ends. The hooks might both be the same size or they might be different sizes—either option will work for your rubber band projects. When choosing a double-ended crochet hook, be sure that the hooks are size G, H, I, or J (4–6mm). Also make sure your bands will slide easily along the length of the hook.

Loop holder: This is anything that can temporarily hold some of your rubber band loops while you work on the rest of the motif. I use a second crochet hook for this, but you can use a stitch marker, pencil, straw, or anything else you have on hand that works for you.

Locking stitch markers: You will need several locking stitch markers that clip closed for these projects. Two is a good number to have on hand before you get started. You will use these to save your project in case you make a mistake.

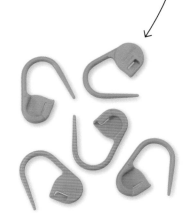

Beads, buttons, charms, and embellishments: You can add a ton of different embellishments to these projects! When choosing beads and embellishments, make sure the holes are large enough to fit your rubber bands. Both sides of a rubber band will fit through a size 6 seed bead and larger. The more bands you are threading through an embellishment, the bigger the hole must be. Check that the bead hole fits the required number of bands before you start your project.

Closures: There are many types of closures you can use depending on your personal preference and the way you'd like your finished project to look. For a quick finish, attach a plastic clip, like an S or C clip, to the first foundation band and the last band of your project. For a more polished look, you can use jewelry pliers and jump rings to attach metal jewelry clasps to the first foundation band and last band of your project.

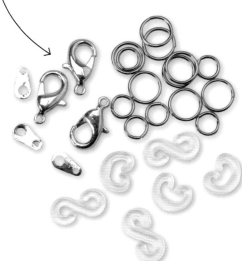

Breaking the Code!

The motifs are made using a set of techniques that are repeated in different combinations. The instructions list the techniques used to make each motif in an abbreviated form—you can think of it as a code. Once you understand the techniques and the code, you will be able to make each motif quickly and easily!

If you get stuck while making a motif, you can always refer back to this section to refresh yourself on a particular technique or code word. The abbreviations are listed in alphabetical order for easy reference later. Don't worry if you see some unfamiliar words here. By the time you get to the end, you will have learned all the new vocabulary!

B = Band

This abbreviation will almost always be paired with a number to tell you what band you are working in the motif. For example B1 means band 1, B2 means band 2, etc. The front end of a band is the end you pull through loops on your hook. The back end is the end you hold in place on your finger until the instructions tell you to put it on the hook.

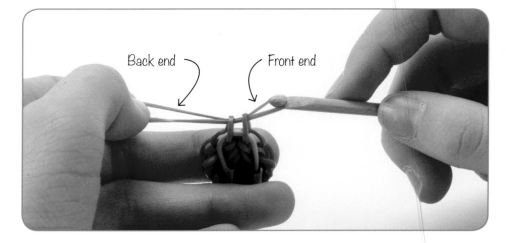

Back end   Front end

Bead

This is an action. Use thread to pull the indicated number of loops through the hole of your chosen bead, button, charm, or embellishment. This means you will remove the loops from the hook and then put them back on again after beading. This is why the thread method works better than your fingers.

Feed one end of the thread through the loops you need to bead.

Feed both ends of the thread through the bead.

Use the thread to pull the loops off the hook, through the bead, and then return them to the hook. Remove the thread.

TIP: After you work a few beginner motifs, the abbreviations will start to feel completely natural—a lot like reading or writing a text message (lol)!

Bind off

With two loops on the working end of the hook, pick up and pass the second loop over the first loop and then over the end of the hook. Keep the first loop on the hook while doing this. This will leave just one loop on the hook.

Pick up the second loop and pass it over the first loop and the end of the hook.

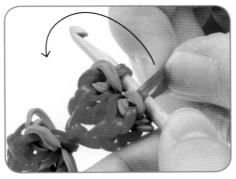

You will be left with one loop on the hook.

BOH = Band on hook

After pulling the front end of a band through the indicated number of loops on your hook, place the back end of the band on the hook.

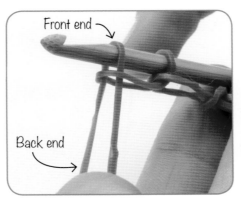

Pull the front end of a band through the indicated number of loops.

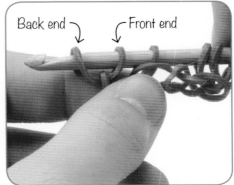

Place the back end of the band on the hook.

C = Color

This abbreviation will almost always be paired with a number to tell you what color band you should be working with. For example C1 means color 1, C2 means color 2, etc.

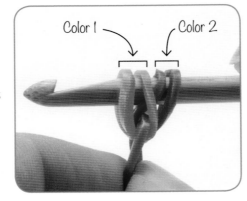

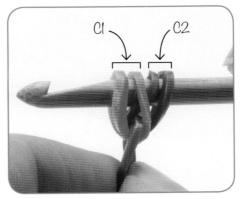

ch = Chain

Create a chain of bands at the beginning and/or end of a project to add extra length. To do this, pull the front end of a band through two loops on the hook. Place the back end of the band on the hook. Repeat until the chain reaches the desired length.

TIP: You can add matching chains to the beginning and end of your project to create a balanced look.

Pull the front end of a band through two loops.

Place the back end of the band on the hook. Repeat.

Cross

Working two bands in two different colors at the same time, pull the front ends through the indicated number of loops on the hook. Place the back ends on the hook. Arrange the four loops on the hook so the loops of the same color are next to each other. You will need to cross the loops on the hook to do this. As you continue the motif, treat the two loops of the same color as one.

Pull two bands in two different colors through the indicated number of loops on the hook.

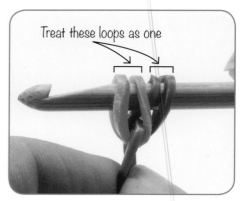

Cross the loops so the loops of the same color are next to each other. Treat the loops of the same color as if they were one loop.

f8 = Figure eight

A figure eight is always used for the first foundation band. Place the front end of a band on the hook. Twist the back end of the band so the two sides cross in the middle, forming a figure eight shape with the band. Place the back end of the band on the hook.

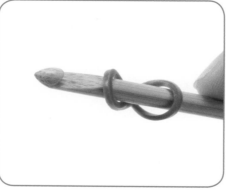

Figure eight as seen from top of hook.

Figure eight as seen from bottom of hook.

FB = Foundation band

This is a band you need to start the first motif, but you will never repeat it in the following motifs.

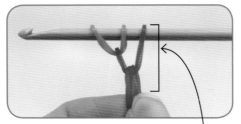

The pink bands are the Foundation Bands

PM = Place marker

Slip a locking stitch marker through all the loops on the hook and close it. This acts as a lifeline or a way to keep your work from unraveling if you drop a loop later on. You will also use the markers to mark stitches you will need to identify later on as you make the motif.

Slip a locking stitch marker through all the loops on the hook and close it.

PT = Pull through

Place the front end of a band on the hook. Hold the back end on your finger while using the hook to pull the front end through the indicated number of loops on the hook. PT1 means you should pull the front end through one loop on the hook; PT2 means you should pull the front end through two loops on the hook, etc. PT is always followed by BOH!

Place the front end of a band on the hook. Hold the back end with your fingers.

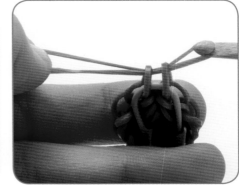

Pull the front end through the indicated number of loops on the hook, causing the loops to slide off the hook onto the band.

ret = Return

Place loops you temporarily moved to the loop holder back on the working end of the hook. In these photos, the loop holder is a double-ended crochet hook, but you can use something else if you like.

Loop holder

Thread the hook you are working with through the loops you temporarily moved to the loop holder.

Remove the loop holder, keeping the loops in place on the hook.

S&T = Slide & turn

Slide all the loops on the hook from the working end to the back end. Then turn the hook so the back end becomes the working end. Note: If you are right handed, the working end of the crochet hook will always be the left end, so you would slide the loops from the left end to the right end, and then turn the hook so the right end becomes the left end. If you are left handed, it would be the other way around.

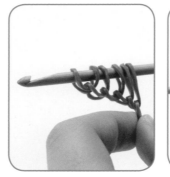

Before sliding and turning, the loops will be at the working end of your hook.

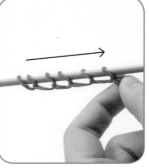

Slide the loops from the working end of the hook to the back end.

Turn the hook around so the back end becomes the working end.

sl = Slip

Remove the indicated number of loops from the working end of the hook and temporarily place them on a loop holder. In these photos, the loop holder is a double-ended crochet hook, but you can use something else if you like.

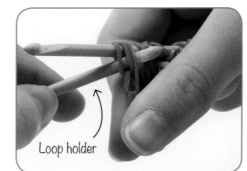

Thread the loop holder through the loops you need to slip.

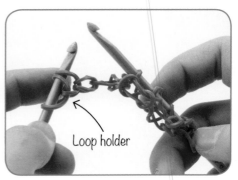

Remove the hook, keeping the loops in place on the loop holder.

WE = Working end

The end of the hook you are using to hook bands. If you are right handed, the working end will always be the left end. If you are left handed, the working end will always be the right end.

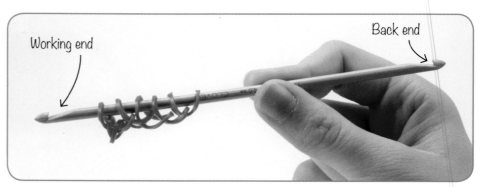

If you are right handed, the working end is the left end of the hook, and the back end is the right end.

Understanding the Diagrams

Each motif includes diagrams that are a visual map of the instructions. Take a look at these diagrams for the Baby Leaf motif so you can learn how to read and follow them.

TIP: A diagram's colors can help you follow along! The foundation bands are always shown in purple. The rest of the bands alternate colors between dark blue and light blue to help you tell them apart.

The labels along the sides of the diagram tell you what band you are looking at. While you read the instructions from top to bottom, you read the diagrams from bottom to top. See how the bottommost bands in the diagram are the foundation bands?

The bands in the diagram do exactly what the instructions say. See how the first foundation band is in the shape of a figure eight? See how the second foundation band is pulled through two loops, and band 1 is pulled through one loop?

Slide and turn (S&T).

Every time you slide and turn (S&T) the bands on the hook, you reverse the design so you can work on the other side. See how diagram 2 is the reverse of diagram 1?

See how adding band 2 and band 3 completes the other side of the design? Once a motif is completed, you can repeat it by placing a stitch marker (PM) through all the loops on the hook (in this case, two) and repeating the indicated steps.

Focus on the new, colored bands in each diagram. Gray bands show the steps you've already completed.

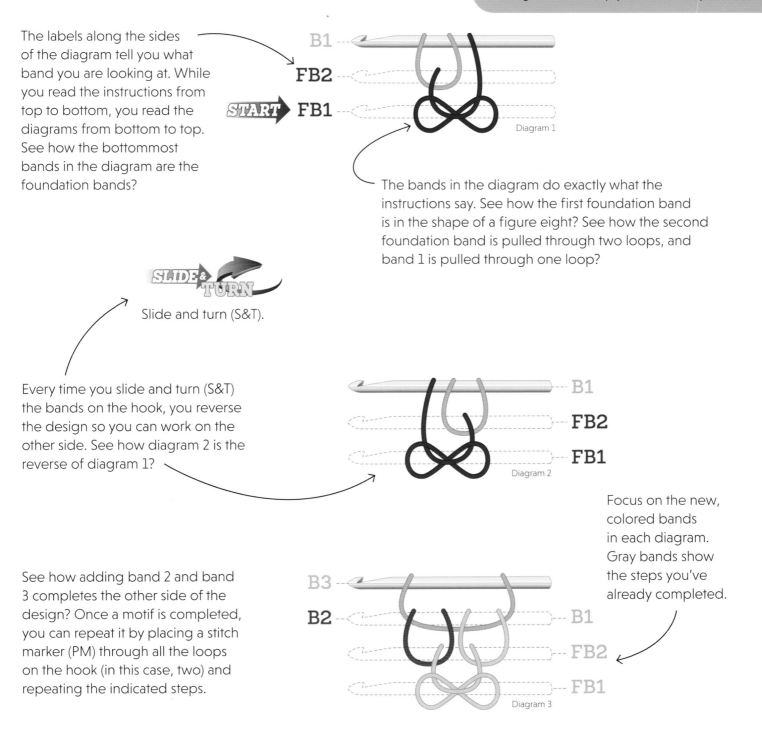

B1
FB2
START FB1
Diagram 1

SLIDE & TURN

B1
FB2
FB1
Diagram 2

B3
B2
B1
FB2
FB1
Diagram 3

Construction & Variations

As you get more and more experienced with the techniques in this book, you might want to begin experimenting with the motifs to make them in different colors, put them together in different combinations, or add embellishments to match your taste. Here are some things to keep in mind as you launch into experimenting with these designs.

Construction: All projects start with a figure eight (f8) band, and some have additional foundation bands (FB). These will be listed in the instructions and shown on the diagrams. Remember to always start a project with the appropriate foundation bands.

Some motifs, such as the Full Shell (page 32) and Palm Leaf (page 36), are made starting at the top of the motif and working down. Others, such as the Embellishment Border (page 39), are made starting at the bottom and working up. Keep this in mind if you're experimenting with combining different motifs in one project.

After you complete a motif, always put a place marker (PM)—a stitch marker—through all of the loops on the hook and close it. The marker will keep anything below it from unraveling, so if you drop a loop as you are making the next motif, the rest of your work will be safe. If you do drop a loop and your work unravels, undo everything down to the stitch marker. Then put the loops on the stitch marker back on your hook and start from there. Don't forget to move the stitch marker up every time you complete a motif.

Color variations: Many motifs are accompanied by color variations. These list the colors you need to use for each band in the motif to create a particular color pattern. Special instructions are also included where necessary. Follow these special instructions carefully so you can make sure the colors appear where you want them to in the design.

Design variations: Most variations are based on color, but some will show you how to add beads, buttons, and/or embellishments, too!

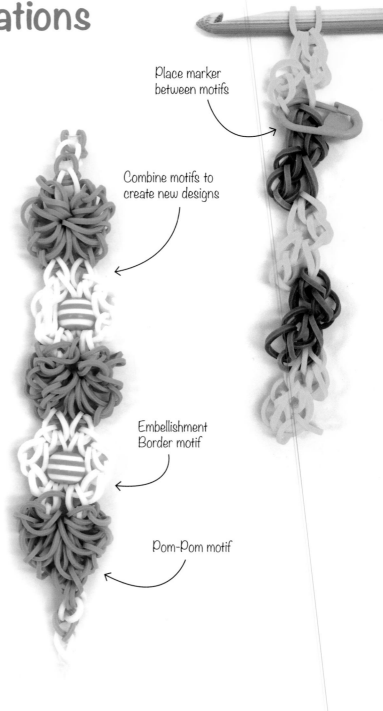

Place marker between motifs

Combine motifs to create new designs

Embellishment Border motif

Pom-Pom motif

Experiment: There are tons of things you can do to alter a motif or create new designs! Try making individual motifs as charms, and then attach them to another rubber band project or a simple chain. Try making Grapes (a variation of the Strawberries motif, page 34) and adding them to the Vining Leaves motif (page 27) to make Vining Grapes. See how many other ideas you can come up with to make new designs!

Making Projects

The motifs in this book can be repeated or attached to chains of bands to make a variety of different projects, including bracelets, book bands, headbands, and necklaces. Refer to this section for information about turning a motif into the project you want.

Palm Leaf (page 36)

For a bracelet: Measure around your wrist and subtract 1" (2.5cm). This is the finished length for your bracelet. Work a motif. Repeat the motif as many times as necessary to reach the finished length (see page 7). To finish, put a closure on the first foundation band (FB1) and the last band of the last motif, being careful not to twist the bracelet.

Half Shell (page 29)

For a headband: Measure from the bottom of your left ear over the top of your head to the bottom of your right ear. Take this measurement and subtract 1" (2.5cm). This is the finished length for the top of your headband. Work a motif. Repeat the motif as many times as necessary to reach the finished length for the top of the headband (see page 7). Working from the last motif, make a chain of bands for the bottom of the headband using the following pattern: PT2, BOH. Repeat until the chain is long enough for the headband to fit comfortably around your head. To finish, put a closure on the first foundation band (FB1) and the last band of the chain, being careful not to twist the headband.

For a book band: A book band is a circle that you can use to hold a book closed or as a bookmark. Measure the height of your book cover and subtract 1" (2.5cm). This is the cover length for your book band. Work a motif. Repeat the motif as many times as necessary to reach the cover length (see page 7). Working from the last motif, make a chain of bands using the following pattern: PT2, BOH. Repeat until the chain reaches the cover length. Make sure the band fits comfortably around your book before finishing. Finish as with the bracelet or headband.

For the headband and book band: After the figure eight band (f8), chain (ch) two or three bands and then continue with the remaining foundation bands (FB) and motif pattern. This will help hide your clasp in the finished project, giving it a more polished look. Include these optional beginning chains as part of the total chain measurement.

Palm Leaf variation: Christmas Tree (page 38)

For a necklace: You do not want your necklace to be tight around your neck (safety first!) so make sure the finished length is longer than the measurement around your neck. Decide how long you'd like your necklace to be. If you're having trouble deciding, try draping a flexible tape measure around your neck like a necklace to see what different lengths look like. Work a motif. Repeat the motif as many times as necessary to reach the desired length (see page 7). Finish as with the bracelet or headband (see page 17). The Embellishment Border motif makes a beautiful necklace, and the Circular Pendant motif includes specific instructions for creating a pendant necklace with that motif (see page 46).

Embellishment Border (page 39)

Baby Leaf

DIFFICULTY LEVEL: Beginner
GAUGE: ½" (1.5cm) per motif

Instructions

To help you familiarize yourself with the abbreviated instructions (the code), this first project has the instructions written out with the technique abbreviations in parentheses. If you are stuck with a particular technique, refer back to page 10 to see photos of how the technique is done.

FB1: Figure eight (f8)
FB2: Pull through two (PT2), band on hook (BOH)
B1: Pull through one (PT1), band on hook (BOH)
Slide and turn (S&T)
B2: Pull through one (PT1), band on hook (BOH)
B3: Pull through all four loops on the hook (PT4), band on hook (BOH)

To repeat the motif, place a stitch marker (PM) through both loops on the hook and repeat the steps for band 1–band 3 (B1–B3). Don't forget to slide and turn (S&T) after band 1 (B1). Repeat as many times as necessary to reach the desired length. See pages 17–18 for information about turning this motif into a bracelet, book band, headband, or necklace. Finish with a plastic clip or jewelry clasp.

Baby Leaf (Continued)

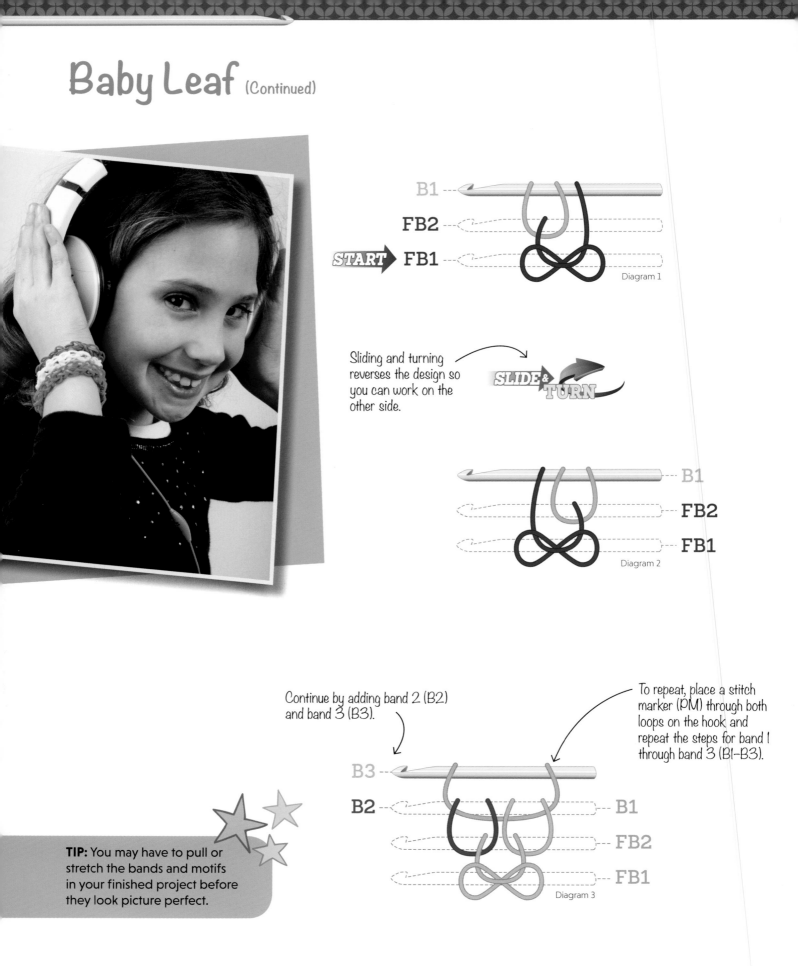

B1

FB2

START ▸ FB1

Diagram 1

Sliding and turning reverses the design so you can work on the other side.

SLIDE & TURN

B1

FB2

FB1

Diagram 2

Continue by adding band 2 (B2) and band 3 (B3).

To repeat, place a stitch marker (PM) through both loops on the hook and repeat the steps for band 1 through band 3 (B1–B3).

B3

B2

B1

FB2

FB1

Diagram 3

TIP: You may have to pull or stretch the bands and motifs in your finished project before they look picture perfect.

Rainy Day

DIFFICULTY LEVEL: Beginner
GAUGE: ½" (1.5cm) per motif

MATERIALS

- 4 foundation bands
- 6 bands per motif
- Double-ended crochet hook
- 1 locking stitch marker

TECHNIQUES & ABBREVIATIONS

- **B:** Band
- **BOH:** Band on hook
- **f8:** Figure eight
- **FB:** Foundation band
- **PM:** Place marker
- **PT:** Pull through
- **S&T:** Slide & turn

Instructions

FB1: f8
FB2: PT2, BOH
FB3: PT1, BOH
FB4: PT2, BOH
S&T

B1: PT2, BOH
B2: PT2, BOH
S&T

B3: PT2, BOH
B4: PT2, BOH
S&T

B5: PT2, BOH
B6: PT2, BOH

To repeat the motif, PM, S&T, and repeat the steps for B1–B6. Don't forget to S&T after B2, B4, and B6.

Repeat as many times as necessary to reach the desired length. See pages 17–18 for information about turning this motif into a bracelet, book band, headband, or necklace. To end, pull B6 of the last motif through all three loops on the hook and BOH. Finish with a plastic clip or jewelry clasp.

Rainy Day (Continued)

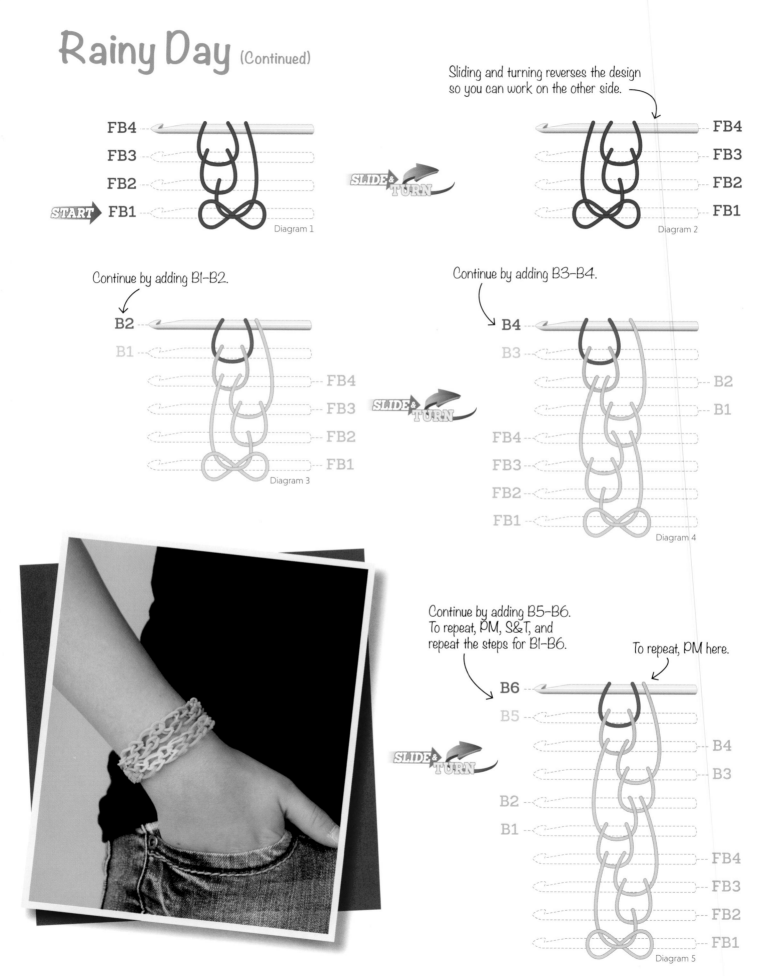

Sliding and turning reverses the design so you can work on the other side.

FB4
FB3
FB2
START → FB1

Diagram 1

SLIDE & TURN

FB4
FB3
FB2
FB1

Diagram 2

Continue by adding B1–B2.

B2
B1
FB4
FB3
FB2
FB1

Diagram 3

SLIDE & TURN

Continue by adding B3–B4.

B4
B3
B2
B1
FB4
FB3
FB2
FB1

Diagram 4

Continue by adding B5–B6.
To repeat, PM, S&T, and repeat the steps for B1–B6.

To repeat, PM here.

B6
B5
B4
B3
B2
B1
FB4
FB3
FB2
FB1

SLIDE & TURN

Diagram 5

Variations

Lay out the bands for your selected variation in order according to the color chart below. Then, follow the instructions to make the motif, picking up the bands in order as you work. This way you don't have to flip back and forth between the instructions and the charts!

Raindrops

BAND	COLOR
FB1	Black
FB2	Black
FB3	Blue
FB4	Black
B1	Blue
B2	Black
B3	Blue
B4	Black
B5	Blue
B6	Black

TIP: After working the two black foundation bands, simply alternate between blue and black bands for the length of the project.

Different Colors

Work each motif in a different color.

Alternating Colors

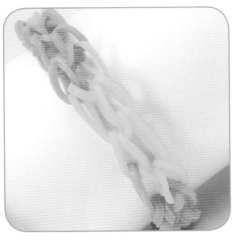

Select two or three colors and alternate them with each motif to create color patterns like C1, C2, C1, C2 (shown) or C1, C2, C3, etc.

Rolling Waves

DIFFICULTY LEVEL: Beginner
GAUGE: ⅞" (2cm) per motif

MATERIALS

- 2 foundation bands
- 6 bands per motif
- Double-ended crochet hook
- 1 locking stitch marker

TECHNIQUES & ABBREVIATIONS

- **B:** Band
- **BOH:** Band on hook
- **f8:** Figure eight
- **FB:** Foundation band
- **PM:** Place marker
- **PT:** Pull through
- **S&T:** Slide & turn

TIP: This pattern is very repetitive. After you work your foundation bands, you can just chant *1, 2, 3, S&T* as you work!

Instructions

FB1: f8
FB2: PT2, BOH
B1: PT1, BOH
B2: PT2, BOH
B3: PT3 (all loops on hook), BOH
S&T
B4: PT1, BOH
B5: PT2, BOH
B6: PT3 (all loops on hook), BOH

To repeat the motif, PM, S&T, and repeat the steps for B1–B6. Don't forget to S&T after B3 and B6. Repeat as many times as necessary to reach the desired length. See pages 17–18 for information about turning this motif into a bracelet, book band, headband, or necklace. Finish with a plastic clip or jewelry clasp.

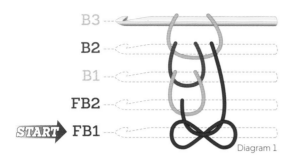

B3
B2
B1
FB2
START FB1

Diagram 1

To repeat, PM here.

B6
B5
B4

B3
B2
B1
FB2
FB1

Diagram 2

Continue by adding B4–B6. To repeat, PM, S&T, and repeat the steps for B1–B6.

Variations

Lay out the bands for your selected variation in order according to the color charts below. Then, follow the instructions to make the motif, picking up the bands in order as you work. This way you don't have to flip back and forth between the instructions and the charts!

Rainbow 1

Rainbow 2

BAND	COLOR
FB1 & FB2	Red
B1	Red
B2	Orange
B3	Yellow
B4	Light green
B5	Light blue
B6	Purple

Repeat color order for each motif throughout.

BAND	COLOR
FB1 & FB2	White
B1	Red
B2	Orange
B3	White
B4	Yellow
B5	Light green
B6	White
B1	Light blue
B2	Purple
B3	White

Repeat color order for each motif throughout.

Rolling Waves (Continued)

Color Blocked Rainbow

BAND	COLOR
FB1 & FB2	Red
Motif 1, B1–B5	Red
Motif 1, B6	Orange
Motif 2, B1–B5	Orange
Motif 2, B6	Yellow
Motif 3, B1–B5	Yellow
Motif 3, B6	Light green
Motif 4, B1–B5	Light green
Motif 4, B6	Light blue
Motif 5, B1–B5	Light blue
Motif 5, B6	Purple
Motif 6, B1–B6	Purple

This number of motifs will make a bracelet 5¼" (13.5cm) long. Add or remove motifs as needed for your desired design.

Half Two-Color Blocking

BAND	COLOR
FB1 & FB2	Light green
B1–B2	Light green
B3–B5	Light blue
B6–B2	Light green
B3–B5	Light blue

Continue to alternate colors every three bands.

Full Two-Color Blocking

Work FB1–FB2 and B1–B5 in one color. Then work B6–B5 in a second color. Continue to alternate colors for each B6–B5 throughout.

Half Three-Color Blocking

Work FB1–FB2 and B1–B2 in one color, work B3–B5 in a second color, and work B6–B2 in a third color. Then continue the color pattern, changing colors every three bands.

Three Color

Alternate three colors every band consistently throughout the project. For example: FBs Red, B1 Red, B2 White, B3 Blue, B4 Red, B5 White, B6 Blue, B1 Red, etc.

Vining Leaves

DIFFICULTY LEVEL: Beginner
GAUGE: 1" (2.5cm) per motif

MATERIALS

- 1 foundation band
- 7 bands per motif
- Double-ended crochet hook
- 1 locking stitch marker
- Thread (optional, to add charms)

TECHNIQUES & ABBREVIATIONS

- **B:** Band
- **BOH:** Band on hook
- **f8:** Figure eight
- **FB:** Foundation band
- **PM:** Place marker
- **PT:** Pull through
- **S&T:** Slide & turn

Instructions

FB: f8
B1: PT2, BOH
B2: PT1, BOH
B3: PT1, BOH

S&T

B4: PT1, BOH
B5: PT1, BOH
B6: PT6 (all loops on hook), BOH
B7: PT2, BOH

To repeat the motif, PM and repeat the steps for B1–B7. Don't forget to S&T after B3. Repeat as many times as necessary to reach the desired length. See pages 17–18 for information about turning this motif into a bracelet, book band, headband, or necklace. Finish with a plastic clip or jewelry clasp.

Vining Leaves (Continued)

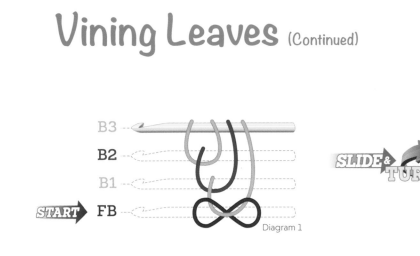

Diagram 1

SLIDE & TURN

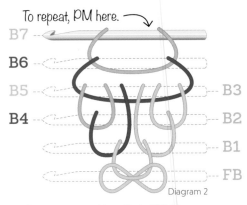

To repeat, PM here.

Diagram 2

Continue by adding B4–B7. To repeat, PM and repeat the steps for B1–B7.

TIP: Try adding charms to your vine as you work! To do this, bead a charm on B7 before placing it on the hook. Then, work B7 as directed. The charm will hang down from the B7 band in the motif. You can use store-bought charms and embellishments for this, or pre-made single motifs like Strawberries or Grapes.

Half Shell

DIFFICULTY LEVEL: Intermediate
GAUGE: 1" (2.5cm) per motif

MATERIALS

- 2 foundation bands
- 10 bands per motif
- Double-ended crochet hook
- 1 locking stitch marker

TECHNIQUES & ABBREVIATIONS

- **B:** Band
- **BOH:** Band on hook
- **f8:** Figure eight
- **FB:** Foundation band
- **PM:** Place marker
- **PT:** Pull through
- **S&T:** Slide & turn

Instructions

FB1: f8
FB2: PT2, BOH
B1: PT1, BOH
B2: PT1, BOH
B3: PT1, BOH
B4: PT1, BOH
B5: PT6 (all loops on hook), BOH
S&T
B6: PT1, BOH
B7: PT1, BOH
B8: PT1, BOH
B9: PT1, BOH
B10: PT6 (all loops on hook), BOH

To repeat the motif, PM, S&T, and repeat the steps for B1–B10. Don't forget to S&T after B5 and B10. Repeat as many times as necessary to reach the desired length. See pages 17–18 for information about turning this motif into a bracelet, book band, headband, or necklace. Finish with a plastic clip or jewelry clasp.

TIP: Stay organized and keep track of where you are in a motif by counting out your bands ahead of time. For the Half Shell motif, lay out your two foundation bands, and then count out piles of ten bands for each motif. Work from one pile at a time for each motif.

Half Shell (Continued)

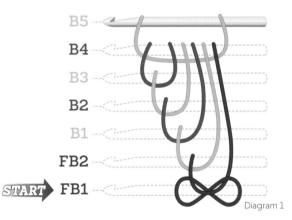

Diagram 1

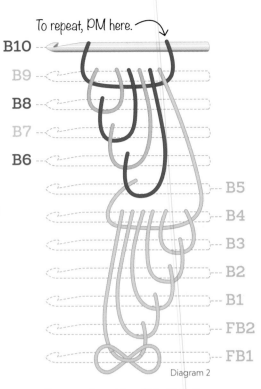

To repeat, PM here.

Diagram 2

Continue by adding B6–B10. To repeat, PM, S&T, and repeat the steps for B1–B10.

Variations

Lay out the bands for your selected variation in order according to the color charts at the right. Then, follow the instructions to make the motif, picking up the bands in order as you work. This way you don't have to flip back and forth between the instructions and the charts!

Rainbow

BAND	COLOR
FB1 & FB2	Red
B1	Pink
B2	Yellow
B3	Light green
B4	Light blue
B5	Red
B6	Pink
B7	Yellow
B8	Light green
B9	Light blue
B10	Red

Repeat color order for each motif throughout.

Half Two-Color Blocking

BAND	COLOR
FB1 & FB2	Light green
B1–B4	Light green
B5–B9	Light blue
B10–B4	Light green
B5–B9	Light blue

Continue to alternate colors every five bands.

Color Blocked Rainbow

BAND	COLOR
FB1 & FB2	Red
Motif 1, B1–B9	Red
Motif 1, B10	Orange
Motif 2, B1–B9	Orange
Motif 2, B10	Yellow
Motif 3, B1–B9	Yellow
Motif 3, B10	Light green
Motif 4, B1–B9	Light green
Motif 4, B10	Light blue
Motif 5, B1–B9	Light blue
Motif 5, B10	Purple
Motif 6, B1–B10	Purple

This number of motifs will make a bracelet 6" (15cm) long. Add or remove motifs as needed for your desired design.

Full Two-Color Blocking

Work FB1–B9 in one color. Then work B10–B9 in a second color. Continue to alternate colors for each B10–B9 throughout.

Half Three-Color Blocking

Work FB1–B4 in red, B5–B9 in pink, and B10–B4 in white. Then continue the color pattern, changing colors every five bands.

Three Color

Alternate three colors every band consistently throughout the project. For example: FBs Red, B1 Red, B2 White, B3 Blue, B4 Red, B5 White, B6 Blue, B7 Red, etc.

Full Shell

DIFFICULTY LEVEL: Intermediate
GAUGE: ¾" (2cm) per motif

MATERIALS

- 1 foundation band
- 10 bands per motif
- 10 size 6 seed beads per motif (optional, for Sugar Rush variation)
- Double-ended crochet hook
- Loop holder (optional, for Sugar Rush variation)
- 1 locking stitch marker
- Thread (optional, for Sugar Rush variation)

TECHNIQUES & ABBREVIATIONS

- **B:** Band
- **Bead:** Thread the indicated number of loops through the hole of your chosen embellishment
- **BOH:** Band on hook
- **f8:** Figure eight
- **FB:** Foundation band
- **PM:** Place marker
- **PT:** Pull through
- **ret:** Return slipped loops to hook
- **S&T:** Slide & turn
- **sl:** Slip loops from hook
- **WE:** Working end

TIP: When beading, make sure your loops are secure on your thread *before* you remove them from your hook. You could even secure them with a stitch marker so they don't accidentally fall away.

Instructions

FB: f8
B1: PT2, BOH
B2: PT1, BOH
For Sugar Rush variation: sl 1, bead 1 pink bead on first loop of WE, ret 1
B3: PT1, BOH
For Sugar Rush variation: sl 1, bead 1 orange bead on first loop of WE, ret 1
B4: PT1, BOH
For Sugar Rush variation: sl 1, bead 1 light green bead on first loop of WE, ret 1
B5: PT1, BOH
For Sugar Rush variation: sl 1, bead 1 blue bead on first loop of WE, ret 1, bead 1 purple bead on returned loop

S&T

B6: PT1, BOH
For Sugar Rush variation: sl 1, bead 1 pink bead on first loop of WE, ret 1
B7: PT1, BOH
For Sugar Rush variation: sl 1, bead 1 orange bead on first loop of WE, ret 1
B8: PT1, BOH
For Sugar Rush variation: sl 1, bead 1 light green bead on first loop of WE, ret 1
B9: PT1, BOH
For Sugar Rush variation: sl 1, bead 1 blue bead on first loop of WE, ret 1, bead 1 purple bead on returned loop
B10: PT10 (all loops on hook), BOH

To repeat the motif, PM and repeat the steps for B1–B10. Don't forget to S&T after B5. Repeat as many times as necessary to reach the desired length. See pages 17–18 for information about turning this motif into a bracelet, book band, headband, or necklace. Finish with a plastic clip or jewelry clasp.

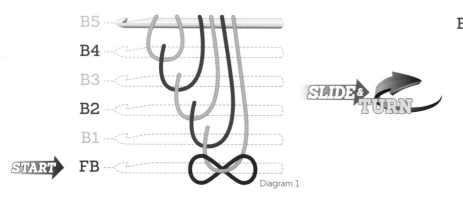

B5
B4
B3
B2
B1

START FB

Diagram 1

SLIDE & TURN

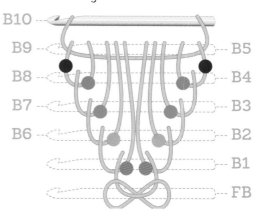

To repeat, PM here.

B10
B9 — B5
B8 — B4
B7 — B3
B6 — B2
— B1
— FB

Diagram 2

Continue by adding B6–B10. To repeat, PM and repeat the steps for B1–B10.

Variations

Lay out the bands for your selected variation in order according to the color charts below. Then, follow the instructions to make the motif, picking up the bands in order as you work. This way you don't have to flip back and forth between the instructions and the charts!

Sugar Rush

BAND	COLOR	BEAD COLOR
FB	White	None
B1	White	None
B2	White	Pink
B3	White	Orange
B4	White	Light green
B5	White	Blue and purple
B6	White	Pink
B7	White	Orange
B8	White	Light green
B9	White	Blue and purple
B10	White	None

Sugar Rush variation

B10
B9 — B5
B8 — B4
B7 — B3
B6 — B2
— B1
— FB

Rainbow

BAND	COLOR
FB	Purple
B1	Purple
B2	Light blue
B3	Light green
B4	Yellow
B5	Red
B6	Light blue
B7	Light green
B8	Yellow
B9	Red
B10	White

Repeat color order for each motif throughout.

Strawberries

DIFFICULTY LEVEL: Intermediate
GAUGE: 1¾" (4.5cm) per motif

TECHNIQUES & ABBREVIATIONS

- **B:** Band
- **Bind off:** Pick up and pass the second loop on the working end of the hook over the first loop and over the end of the hook, leaving just one loop on the hook.
- **BOH:** Band on hook
- **f8:** Figure eight
- **FB:** Foundation band
- **PM:** Place marker
- **PT:** Pull through
- **S&T:** Slide & turn
- **WE:** Working end

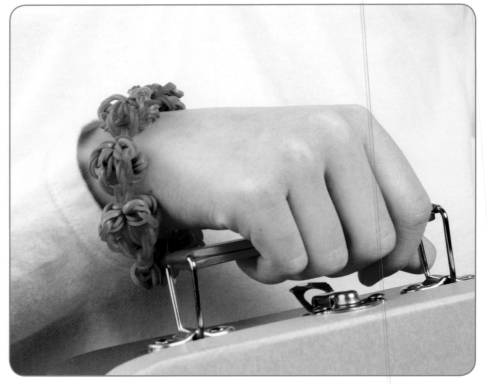

Instructions

With the exception of the foundation band, use two bands as one for every step throughout. For example, for B1, pull two red bands through two loops on the hook for the first motif. Using two bands as one means you will also have doubled loops on your hook. Treat every doubled loop as one.

FB (Red): f8
Don't forget to use two bands as one for each of the next steps, and treat all doubled loops as one loop!
B1 (Red): PT2 for first motif only; for following motifs PT1, BOH
B2 (Red): PT1, BOH
B3 (Green): PT1, BOH

S&T

B4 (Red): PT1, BOH
B5 (Green): PT1, BOH
B6 (Red): PT6 (all loops on hook), BOH

Bind off

Don't forget to use two bands as one for each of the next steps, and treat all doubled loops as one loop!
B7 (Red): PT1, BOH
B8 (Red): PT1, BOH
B9 (Red): PT1, BOH
B10 (Green): PT1, BOH

S&T

B11 (Red): PT1, BOH
B12 (Red): PT1, BOH
B13 (Green): PT1, BOH
B14 (Red): PT8 (all loops on hook), BOH

Bind off

To repeat the motif, PM and repeat the steps for B1–B14, including the second bind off. Don't forget to S&T after B3 and B10 and to bind off after B6 and B14. Repeat as many times as necessary to reach the desired length. See pages 17–18 for information about turning this motif into a bracelet, book band, headband, or necklace. Finish with a plastic clip or jewelry clasp.

TIP: When working this motif, make sure the loop left on the hook after each bind off stitch leans *away* from the working end of your hook. For right handers, bind off loops should always lean to the right.

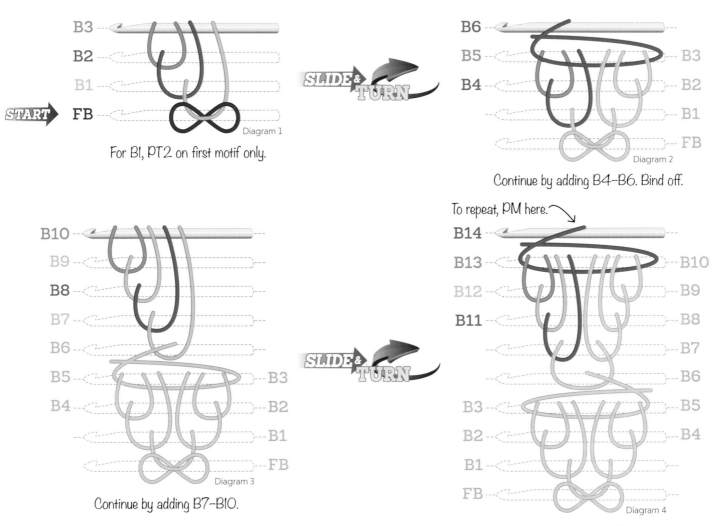

B3
B2
B1
FB

START →

For B1, PT2 on first motif only.

Diagram 1

SLIDE & TURN

B6
B5
B4

B3
B2
B1
FB

Continue by adding B4–B6. Bind off.

Diagram 2

B10
B9
B8
B7
B6
B5
B4

B3
B2
B1
FB

Diagram 3

Continue by adding B7–B10.

SLIDE & TURN

To repeat, PM here.

B14
B13
B12
B11

B10
B9
B8
B7
B6
B5
B4

B3
B2
B1
FB

Diagram 4

Continue by adding B11–B14. Bind off.
To repeat, PM and repeat the steps for B1–B14.

Variations

Grapes

Replace the red bands with purple bands throughout the motif. I made the example shown with knobbed bands that are a little thicker than standard bands, so I did not double the bands like the instructions say. See page 28 to learn how to add Grapes to the Vining Leaves motif.

TIP: This pattern creates two strawberries per motif—a little one and a big one!

TIP: When making charms from Strawberries and Grapes, use green bands for B6 and B14 for a finished look.

Palm Leaf

DIFFICULTY LEVEL: Intermediate
GAUGE: 1" (2.5cm) per motif

MATERIALS

- 1 foundation band
- 22 bands per motif
- Double-ended crochet hook
- Loop holder (optional, for Christmas Tree variation)
- 1 locking stitch marker
- Thread (optional, for Christmas Tree variation)
- Star buttons, 1 for each set of 2 motifs (optional, for Christmas Tree variation)
- Desired number of red and gold size 6 seed beads (optional, for Christmas Tree variation)

TECHNIQUES & ABBREVIATIONS

- **B:** Band
- **Bead:** Thread the indicated number of loops through the hole of your chosen embellishment
- **BOH:** Band on hook
- **ch:** Chain
- **f8:** Figure eight
- **FB:** Foundation band
- **PM:** Place marker
- **PT:** Pull through
- **ret:** Return slipped loops to hook
- **S&T:** Slide & turn
- **sl:** Slip loops from hook
- **WE:** Working end

Instructions

FB: f8	**B11:** PT2, BOH
B1: PT2, BOH	**B12:** PT1, BOH
B2: PT1, BOH	**B13:** PT2, BOH
B3: PT2, BOH	**B14:** PT1, BOH
B4: PT1, BOH	**B15:** PT2, BOH
S&T	**B16:** PT1, BOH
B5: PT1, BOH	**B17:** PT2, BOH
B6: PT2, BOH	**S&T**
B7: PT1, BOH	**B18:** PT1, BOH
B8: PT2, BOH	**B19:** PT2, BOH
B9: PT1, BOH	**B20:** PT1, BOH
B10: PT2, BOH	**B21:** PT2, BOH
S&T	**B22:** PT12 (all loops on hook), BOH

To repeat the motif, PM and repeat the steps for B1-B22. Don't forget to S&T after B4, B10, B17, and sometimes B22 (see tip on page 37). See pages 17–18 for information about turning this motif into a bracelet, book band, headband, or necklace. Repeat as many times as necessary to reach the desired length. Finish with a plastic clip or jewelry clasp.

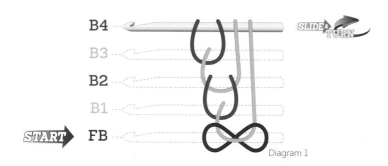

B4

B3

B2

B1

START FB

Diagram 1

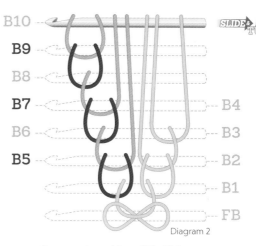

B10

B9

B8

B7 — B4

B6 — B3

B5 — B2

— B1

— FB

Diagram 2

Continue by adding B5–B10.

To repeat, PM here.

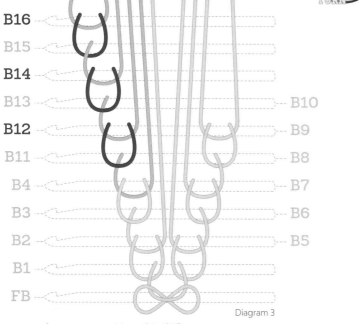

B17

B16

B15

B14

B13

B12

B11

B4 — B10

B3 — B9

B2 — B8

B1 — B7

FB — B6

— B5

Diagram 3

Continue by adding B11–B17.

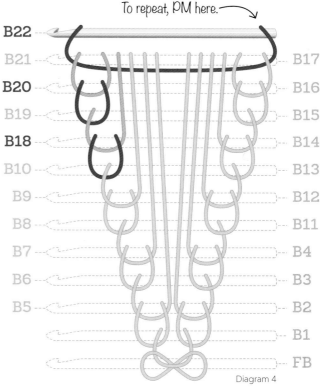

B22

B21 — B17

B20 — B16

B19 — B15

B18 — B14

B10 — B13

B9 — B12

B8 — B11

B7 — B4

B6 — B3

B5 — B2

— B1

— FB

Diagram 4

Continue by adding B18–B22. To repeat, PM and repeat the steps for B1–B22. If adding embellishments to the same side of each motif, S&T after B22 (see tip below).

TIP: If you are adding embellishments to a particular band (or bands) in each motif, S&T after B22 if you want the embellishments to be on the same side of every motif. If you want the embellishments to alternate sides, don't S&T after B22. This applies to all symmertrical motifs.

Palm Leaf (Continued)

Variations

Lay out the bands for your selected variation in order according to the color chart below. Then, follow the instructions to make the motif, picking up the bands in order as you work. This way you don't have to flip back and forth between the instructions and the charts!

Christmas Tree

Work FB and B1–B21 in green/white speckled bands. Work B22 in brown. Bead a star button on B1 of every other motif for an alternating pattern. Between B22 and all B1s with star buttons, ch one additional band in brown (B22, ch 1 in brown, B1 with star button). After the last motif, ch one or more additional bands in brown. If desired, randomly bead red and gold size 6 seed beads onto the bands as you work (sl 1, bead on WE band, ret 1). Try slipping one or more loops to a loop holder to bead loops near the center of your motif, or keep it simple by not slipping any loops and beading the first WE loop only. Use both techniques randomly to achieve the best look.

Campfire

BAND	COLOR
FB	Yellow
B1–B7	Yellow
B8–B13	Orange
B14–B21	Red
B22	Yellow

Repeat color order for each motif throughout.

Using Buttons

There are two different types of buttons—shank buttons and standard buttons. Shank buttons have a stem (or shank) attached to them. To use a shank button in your design, thread your loops through the hole in the shank, just like you would a bead. A standard button is flat and has holes all the way through it. To use a standard button in your design, thread your loops through one of the holes in the button from back to front. Then thread the bands through a different hole from front to back.

For shank buttons, thread your loops through the hole in the shank.

For standard buttons, thread your loops up through one hole and down through another hole.

Embellishment Border

DIFFICULTY LEVEL: Advanced
GAUGE: 1⅜" (3.5cm) per motif

MATERIALS

- 2 foundation bands
- 15 bands per motif
- Double-ended crochet hook
- Loop holder
- 1 locking stitch marker
- 1 bead or button per motif
- Thread or beader

TECHNIQUES & ABBREVIATIONS

- **B:** Band
- **Bead:** Thread the indicated number of loops through the hole of your chosen embellishment
- **BOH:** Band on hook
- **Cross:** Working two bands in two different colors at the same time, pull the front ends through the indicated number of loops on the hook. Place the back ends on the hook. Cross the loops on the hook so the loops of the same color are next to each other. Treat the two loops of the same color as one.
- **f8:** Figure eight
- **FB:** Foundation band
- **PM:** Place marker
- **PT:** Pull through
- **ret:** Return slipped loops to hook
- **S&T:** Slide & turn
- **sl:** Slip loops from hook
- **WE:** Working end

Instructions

FB1: f8
FB2: PT2, BOH
B1: PT1, BOH
B2: PT2, BOH
B3: PT1, BOH
B4: PT2, BOH
B5: PT1, BOH

S&T

B6: PT1, BOH
B7: PT2, BOH
B8: PT1, BOH
B9: PT2, BOH

B10: PT1, BOH
sl 3, bead with next 2 loops on WE, ret 3
B11: PT3, BOH
B12: PT3, BOH

S&T

B13: PT3, BOH
B14: PT3, BOH
B15: PT4 (all loops on hook), BOH

To repeat the motif, PM and repeat the steps for B1–B15. Don't forget to S&T after B5 and B12. Repeat as many times as necessary to reach the desired length. See pages 17–18 for information about turning this motif into a bracelet, book band, headband, or necklace. Finish with a plastic clip or jewelry clasp.

Embellishment Border (Continued)

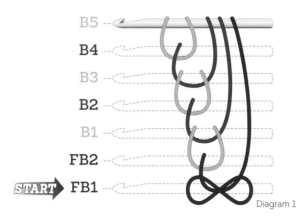

B5
B4
B3
B2
B1
FB2
START FB1

Diagram 1

SLIDE & TURN

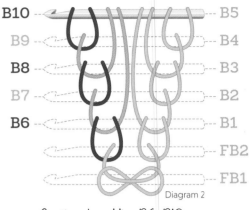

B10 — B5
B9 — B4
B8 — B3
B7 — B2
B6 — B1
— FB2
— FB1

Diagram 2

Continue by adding B6–B10.

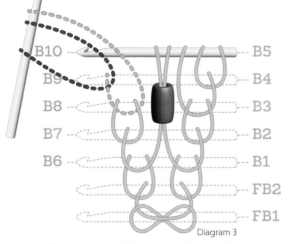

B10 — B5
B9 — B4
B8 — B3
B7 — B2
B6 — B1
— FB2
— FB1

Diagram 3

Continue with sl 3, bead with next 2 loops
on WE, ret 3.

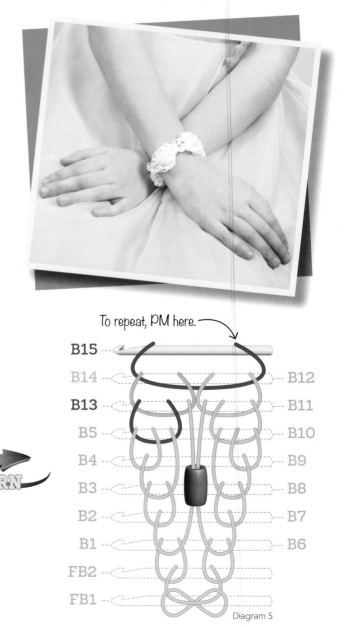

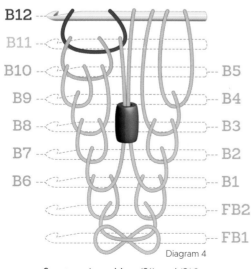

B12
B11
B10 — B5
B9 — B4
B8 — B3
B7 — B2
B6 — B1
— FB2
— FB1

Diagram 4

Continue by adding B11 and B12.

SLIDE & TURN

To repeat, PM here.

B15
B14 — B12
B13 — B11
B5 — B10
B4 — B9
B3 — B8
B2 — B7
B1 — B6
FB2
FB1

Diagram 5

Continue by adding B13–B15. To repeat,
PM and repeat the steps for B1–B15.

Variations

Lay out the bands for your selected variation in order according to the color charts below. Then, follow the instructions to make the motif, picking up the bands in order as you work. This way you don't have to flip back and forth between the instructions and the charts!

Rainbow

BAND	COLOR
FB1 & FB2	Red
B1	Orange
B2	White
B3	Yellow
B4	Light green
B5	Light blue
B6	Orange
B7	White
B8	Yellow
B9	Light green
B10	Light blue
B11	Dark blue
B12	Purple
B13	Dark blue
B14	Purple
B15	Red

Repeat color order for each motif throughout.

Tie-Dye

BAND	COLOR
FB1 & FB2	Red
B1	Pink
B2	Yellow
B3	Green
B4	Blue
B5	Red
B6	Pink
B7	Yellow
B8	Green
B9	Blue
B10	Red
B11	Pink
B12	Yellow
B13	Pink
B14	Yellow
B15	Red

Repeat color order for each motif throughout.

Two-Color Zigzag

BAND	COLOR FOR ODD MOTIFS	COLOR FOR EVEN MOTIFS
FB1	White	
FB2	White and Pink, cross White to WE	
B1	White	Pink
B2	White	Pink
B3	White	Pink
B4	White	Pink
B5	White	Pink
B6	Pink	White
B7	Pink	White
B8	Pink	White
B9	Pink	White
B10	Pink	White
B11	Pink	White
B12	Pink	White
B13	White	Pink
B14	White	Pink
B15	White and Pink, cross Pink to WE	White and Pink, cross White to WE

Repeat color order for each set of motifs throughout.

Pom-Pom

DIFFICULTY LEVEL: Advanced
GAUGE: 1¼" (3cm) per motif

MATERIALS

- 1 foundation band
- 20 bands per motif
- Double-ended crochet hook
- 1 locking stitch marker
- Beads or other embellishments (optional, for Letters variation)
- Thread (optional, for Letters variation)

TECHNIQUES & ABBREVIATIONS

- **B:** Band
- **Bead:** Thread the indicated number of loops through the hole of your chosen embellishment
- **BOH:** Band on hook
- **f8:** Figure eight
- **FB:** Foundation band
- **PM:** Place marker
- **PT:** Pull through
- **S&T:** Slide & turn

Instructions

FB: f8
B1: PT2, BOH (if desired, bead these 2 loops*)
B2–B10: PT1, BOH
S&T

B11–B19: PT1, BOH
B20: PT20 (all loops on hook), BOH

To repeat the motif, PM and repeat the steps for B1–B20. Don't forget to S&T after B10. Repeat as many times as necessary to reach the desired length. See pages 17–18 for information about turning this motif into a bracelet, book band, headband, or necklace. Finish with a plastic clip or jewelry clasp.

TIP: For each motif, count out two piles of nine bands each. Work B2–B10 using the first pile of bands, and then S&T. Work B11–B19 using the second pile of bands. This way, you don't have to count band numbers while you work.

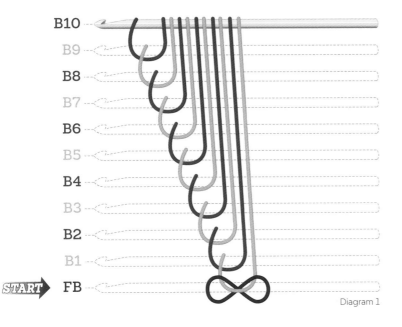

B10
B9
B8
B7
B6
B5
B4
B3
B2
B1
START ➤ FB

Diagram 1

SLIDE & TURN

To repeat, PM here.

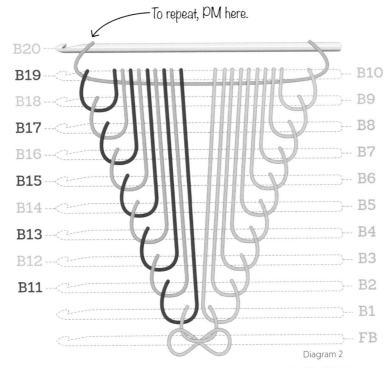

B20
B19 .... B10
B18 .... B9
B17 .... B8
B16 .... B7
B15 .... B6
B14 .... B5
B13 .... B4
B12 .... B3
B11 .... B2
       .... B1
       .... FB

Diagram 2

Continue by adding B11–B20. To repeat, PM and repeat the steps for B1–B20.

Variations

Lay out the bands for your selected variation in order according to the information below. Then, follow the instructions to make the motif, picking up the bands in order as you work. This way you don't have to flip back and forth between the instructions and the color variations!

Peppermints

Use a combination of green and white bands or red and white bands. Work the FB and all odd numbered bands (B1, B3, B5, etc.) in red or green. Work all even numbered bands (B2, B4, B6, etc.) in white.

Team Spirit

Work all odd numbered motifs (1, 3, 5, etc.) in one color and all even numbered motifs (2, 4, 6, etc.) in a second color. Customize the two colors you use to match your team's colors!

Letters

You can add beads to the two loops of B1 of each motif.* Consider using alphabet beads to spell out your team name between pom-poms.

Feather

DIFFICULTY LEVEL: Advanced
GAUGE: 1½" (4cm) per motif

MATERIALS

- 1 foundation band
- 16 bands per motif
- Double-ended crochet hook
- Loop holder
- 1 locking stitch marker
- Thread (optional, for Peacock variation)
- One ½" (1cm) peacock blue bead (optional, for Peacock variation)

TECHNIQUES & ABBREVIATIONS

- **B:** Band
- **Bead:** Thread the indicated number of loops through the hole of your chosen embellishment
- **BOH:** Band on hook
- **f8:** Figure eight
- **FB:** Foundation band
- **PM:** Place marker
- **PT:** Pull through
- **ret:** Return slipped loops to hook
- **S&T:** Slide & turn
- **sl:** Slip loops from hook
- **WE:** Working end

Instructions

FB: f8
B1: PT2, BOH
B2: PT1, BOH
B3: PT2, BOH
S&T

B4: PT1, BOH
B5: PT2, BOH
B6: sl 1, PT2, BOH, ret 1
B7: PT1, BOH
S&T

B8: PT1, BOH
B9: sl 1, PT2, BOH, ret 1
S&T

B10: sl 1, PT2, BOH, ret 1
B11: PT2, BOH
S&T

B12: PT2, BOH
B13: sl 1, PT2, BOH, ret 1
S&T

B14: sl 1, PT2, BOH, ret 1
B15: sl 2, PT2, BOH, ret 2
B16: PT6 (all loops on hook), BOH

To repeat the motif, PM and repeat the steps for B1–B16. Don't forget to S&T after B3, B7, B9, B11, and B13. Repeat as many times as necessary to reach the desired length. See pages 17–18 for information about turning this motif into a bracelet, book band, headband, or necklace. Finish with a plastic clip or jewelry clasp.

Variations

Peacock Feather

Work the entire motif in medium green bands. Work FB and B1–B14 as directed above. Then work B15 as follows: sl 2, PT2, BOH. For the eye, bead the first 2 loops on the WE through a peacock blue bead, ret 2. Work B16 as directed above.

TIP: Some of the bands in these diagrams look longer than they will in real life as you make your project. The diagram bands are stretched a little more so you can clearly see the steps for adding each band.

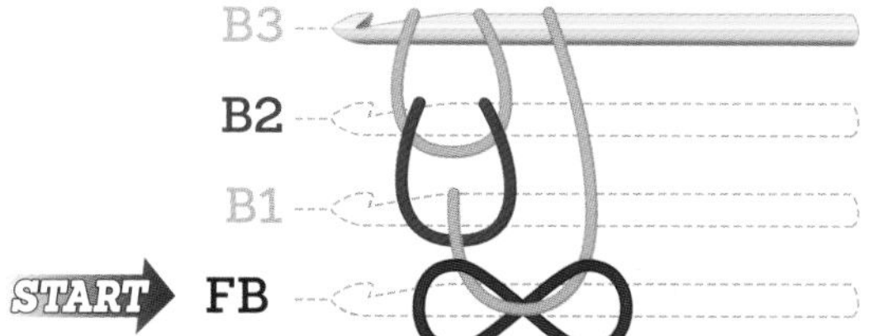

B3
B2
B1
START
FB

Diagram 1

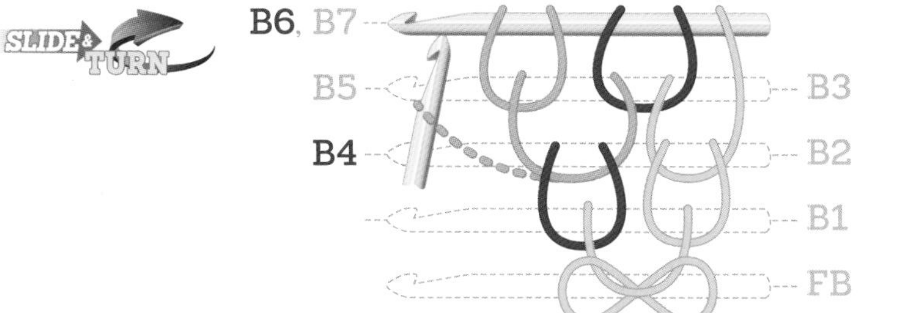

SLIDE & TURN
B6, B7
B5
B4
B3
B2
B1
FB

Diagram 2

Continue by adding B4–B7.

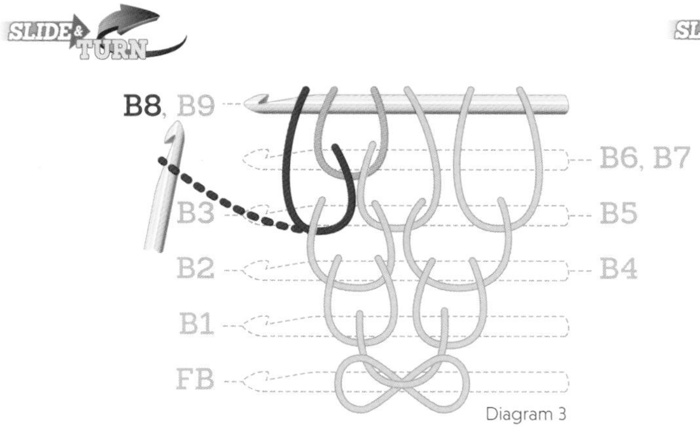

SLIDE & TURN
B8, B9
B6, B7
B3
B5
B2
B4
B1
FB

Diagram 3

Continue by adding B8–B9.

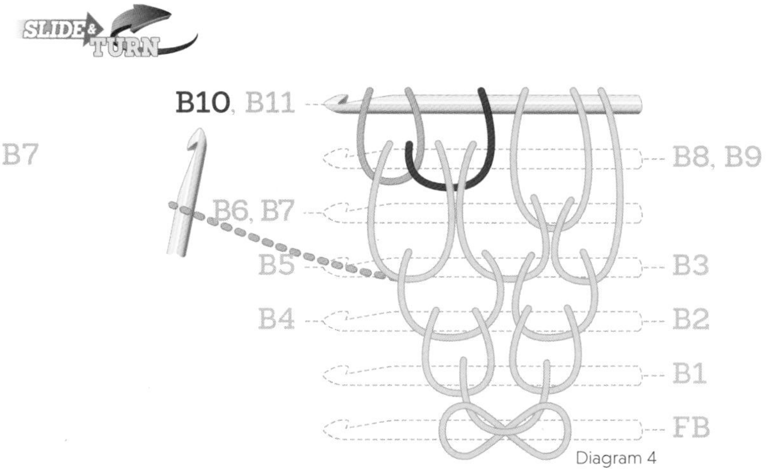

SLIDE & TURN
B10, B11
B8, B9
B6, B7
B5
B3
B4
B2
B1
FB

Diagram 4

Continue by adding B10–B11.

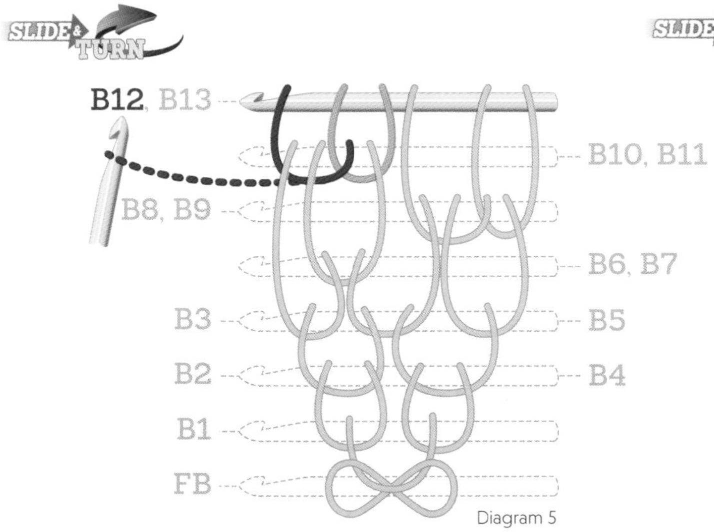

SLIDE & TURN
B12, B13
B10, B11
B8, B9
B6, B7
B3
B5
B2
B4
B1
FB

Diagram 5

Continue by adding B12–B13.

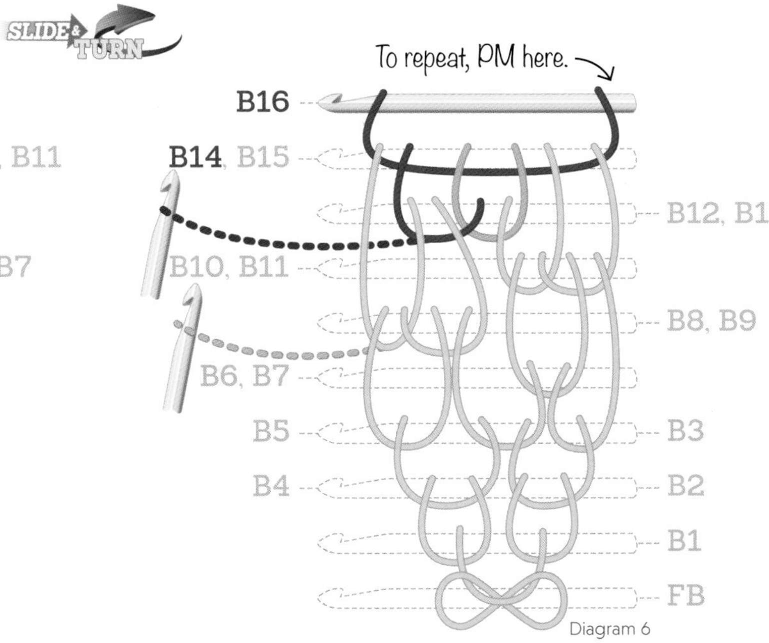

SLIDE & TURN
To repeat, PM here.
B16
B14, B15
B12, B13
B10, B11
B8, B9
B6, B7
B5
B3
B4
B2
B1
FB

Diagram 6

Continue by adding B14–B16.

Circular Pendant

DIFFICULTY LEVEL: Advanced
GAUGE: 1½" (4cm) diameter per pendant

MATERIALS

- 1 foundation band in C1
- 31 bands in C1
- 8 bands in C2
- Additional bands in C1 and C2 for necklace chain (optional)
- Double-ended crochet hook
- 3 locking stitch markers

TECHNIQUES & ABBREVIATIONS

- **B:** band
- **BOH:** Band on hook
- **ch:** Chain
- **f8:** Figure eight
- **FB:** Foundation band
- **PM:** Place marker
- **PT:** Pull through
- **S&T:** Slide & turn
- **WE:** Working end

TIP: For extra security, PM after B20 before continuing on to B21.

Instructions

Work FB–B19 in C1. Work B20–B26 in C2. Work B27–B38 in C1. Work B39 in C2. Work B40–B41 in C1.

FB (C1): f8
B1 (C1): PT2, BOH
B2 (C1): PT1, BOH
B3 (C1): PT1, BOH
B4 (C1): PT2, BOH
B5 (C1): PT1, BOH, PM on this band (see page 47)
B6 (C1): PT1, BOH
B7 (C1): PT2, BOH

S&T

B8 (C1): PT1, BOH
B9 (C1): PT1, BOH
B10 (C1): PT2, BOH
B11 (C1): PT1, BOH, PM on this band (see page 47)
B12 (C1): PT1, BOH
B13 (C1): PT2, BOH

B14 (C1): PT3, BOH
B15 (C1): PT1, BOH
B16 (C1): PT4, BOH

S&T

B17 (C1): PT3, BOH
B18 (C1): PT1, BOH
B19 (C1): PT4, BOH
B20 (C2): PT6 (all loops on hook), BOH
B21 (C2): PT1, BOH
B22 (C2): PT1, BOH
B23 (C2): PT2, BOH

S&T

B24 (C2): PT1, BOH
B25 (C2): PT1, BOH
B26 (C2): PT2, BOH

(continued on page 47)

Marking and picking up the loops

Mark B5 and B11 by clipping the two loops of each band *below* the hook together with a stitch marker. This will hold the bands in a U shape. Continue working through B26, and then find the marked band at the working end of your hook. Turn your work so you are looking at the top instead of the front. Pick up this loop between the "legs" of the chain stitch above it and place it on the hook. Repeat with the marked band at the back end of the hook. You will now have eight loops on the hook. Remove the stitch markers and continue on to B27.

1. Place a stitch marker through the two loops of B5 and B11 (shown in red) below the hook.

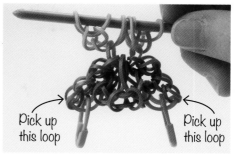

2. Work through B26. Then locate the marked band at the working end of your hook.

3. Turn the work so you're looking at it from the top. Pick up the outside loop of the marked band at the working end of the hook between the "legs" of the chain stitch above it. Place it on the hook.

4. Repeat with the marked band at the back end of the hook. You will have eight loops on the hook. Continue with B27.

Variations

Three Colors

Work B27–B38 in a third color. Return to C2 with B39 as directed at the right.

Pick up loops as directed above.
B27 (C1): PT1, BOH
B28 (C1): PT1, BOH
B29 (C1): PT2, BOH
B30 (C1): PT3, BOH
B31 (C1): PT1, BOH
B32 (C1): PT4, BOH
S&T
B33 (C1): PT1, BOH
B34 (C1): PT1, BOH
B35 (C1): PT2, BOH
B36 (C1): PT3, BOH
B37 (C1): PT1, BOH
B38 (C1): PT4, BOH
B39 (C2): PT8 (all loops on hook), BOH

To repeat, PM and repeat the steps for B1–B39.

To finish the pendant as a necklace:
B40 (C1): PT2, BOH
B41 (C1): PT1, BOH
Alternating between C1 and C2, ch for half the desired length of your necklace chain (PT2, BOH each time, including the first time). Put a closure on the last link of the chain.
S&T

Go back to B40 and PT1, BOH. Alternating between C1 and C2, ch for the other half of the desired length of your necklace chain (PT2, BOH each time, including the first time). Put the last link of the chain on the closure.

Circular Pendant (Continued)

This diagram is read a little bit differently than the others in the book. While the other diagrams show you what you will see on your hook as you work, this diagram shows you the finished motif from the front, so at first, it might seem backwards. Start reading this chart on the left side as you've done previously. Every time you S&T in the instructions, switch to the other side of the chart to follow the loops. For example, start on the left side and follow FB–B7. S&T after B7. When you S&T, switch to the right side of the chart and follow B8–B16. S&T, switch to the left side of the chart, and follow B17–B23, etc. Even though you will be reading from different sides of the chart, you will always work off the working end of your hook (the left end for right handers).

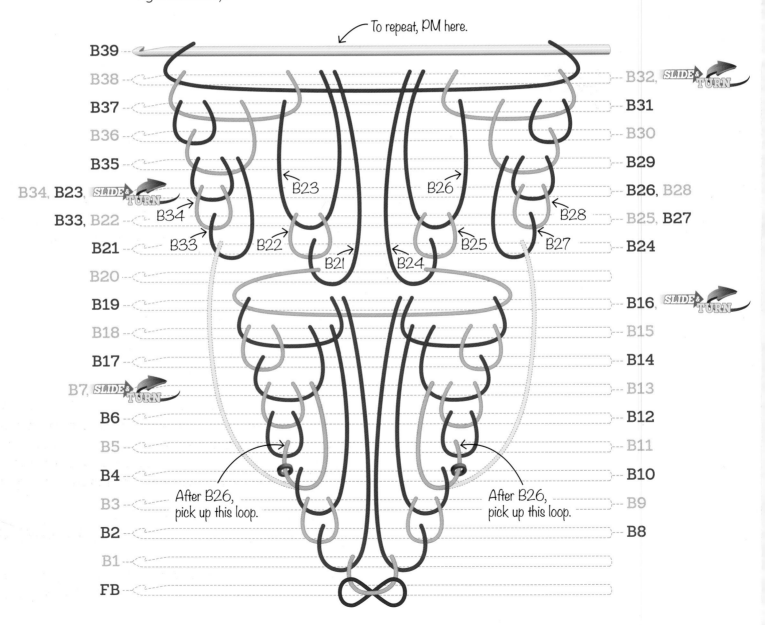